# actual size

## Steve Jenkins

pygmy shrew
5 centimetres long

Frances Lincoln
Children's Books

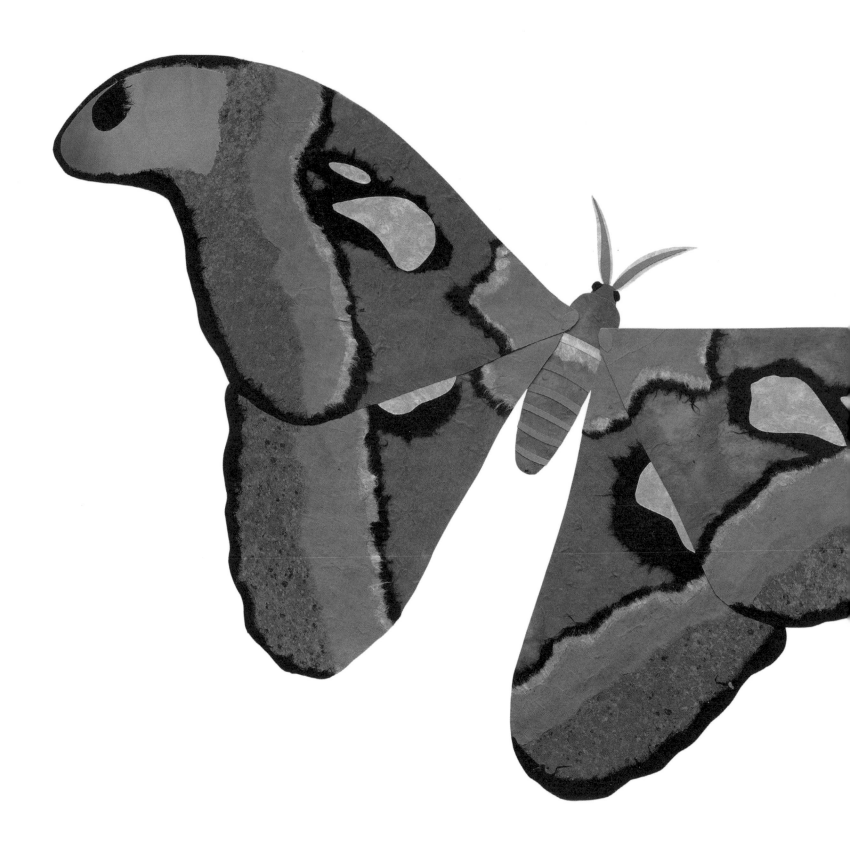

The **atlas moth** is so large that it is
often mistaken for a bird.

wingspan: 30 centimetres

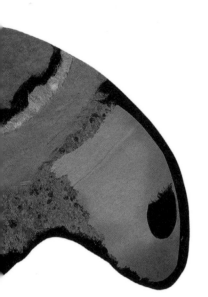

**H**ave you ever looked a giant
squid in the eye? Have you
shaken hands with a gorilla
or been face to face with a tiger?
All the animals in this book are
shown at actual size, so you
can see how you measure up
to creatures both large and small.

The **dwarf goby** is the smallest fish
in the world.

length: 9 millimetres

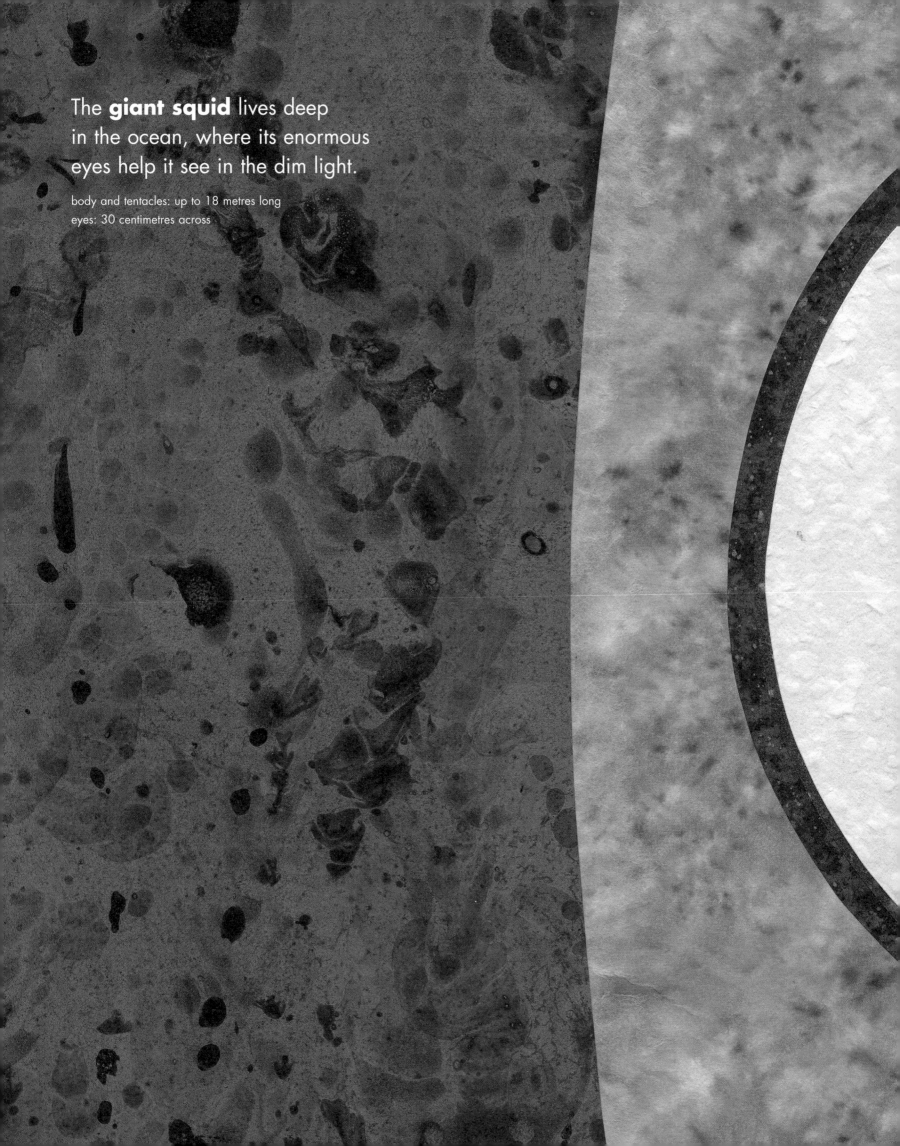

The **giant squid** lives deep
in the ocean, where its enormous
eyes help it see in the dim light.

body and tentacles: up to 18 metres long
eyes: 30 centimetres across

The **Alaskan brown bear** is the largest
meat-eating animal that lives on land.

height: 4 metres    weight: 770 kilograms

Here's the largest bird – an **ostrich** –
with its egg.

height: up to 2·75 metres   weight: 155 kilograms

A 60-centimetre-long tongue!
This must be a **giant anteater**
snacking on its favourite food, termites.

body and tail: 2 metres long    weight: 40 kilograms

The **Goliath birdeater tarantula** is big enough to catch and eat birds and small mammals.

legs: 30 centimetres across

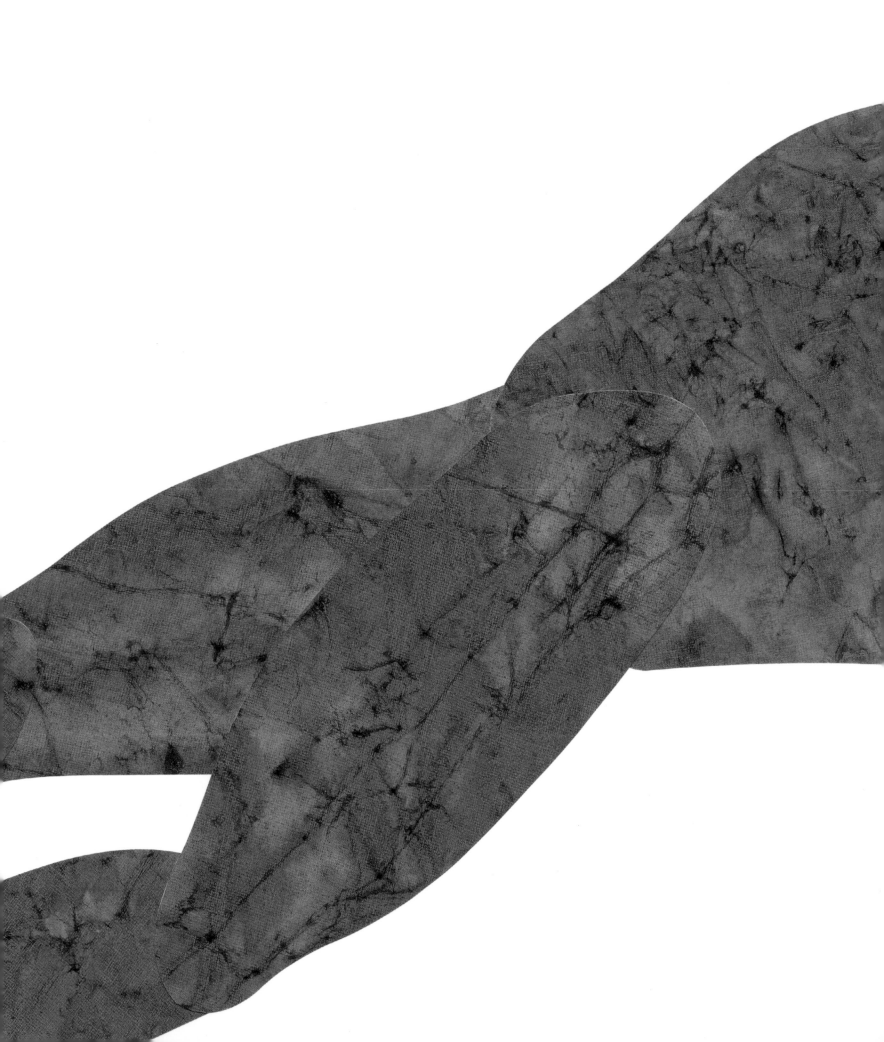

The **Goliath frog** lives in Africa.
It's big enough to catch and eat
birds and rats.

length: 30 centimetres, 90 centimetres with legs extended
weight: 3 kilograms

This is too close to a **great white shark!**

length: 6·5 metres   weight: 2 700 kilograms   teeth: up to 10 centimetres long

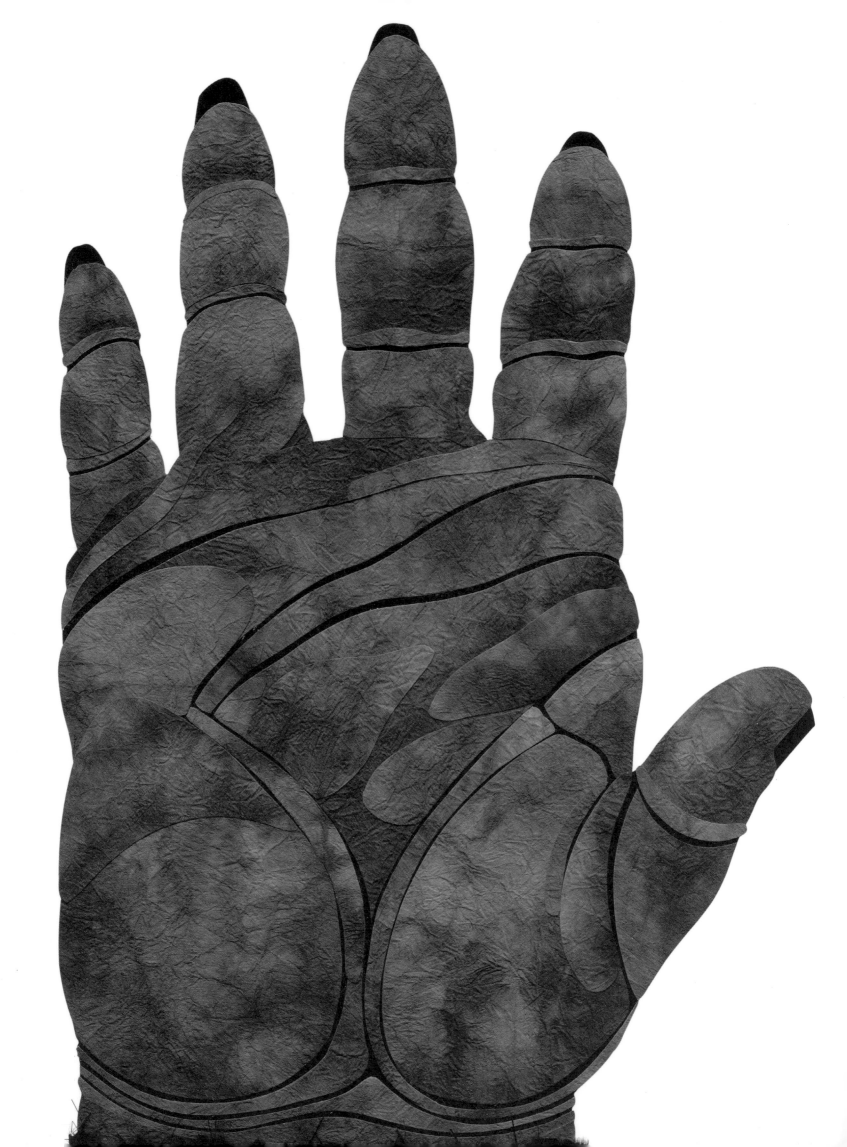

The huge **gorilla** and the **pygmy mouse lemur** both have hands a lot like ours.

gorilla: 1·75 metres tall, 270 kilograms    mouse lemur: 65 millimetres tall, 30 grams

The **Siberian tiger** is the biggest
of the big cats.

length: 4·25 metres, nose to tail    weight: up to 320 kilograms

The **Goliath beetle** is the largest flying insect.

length: 15 centimetres    weight: 100 grams

The rare **giant walking stick**
is the world's longest insect.

length: 56 centimetres

This foot belongs to the largest land animal, the **African elephant**.

height: up to 4 metres
weight: as much as 6 350 kilograms

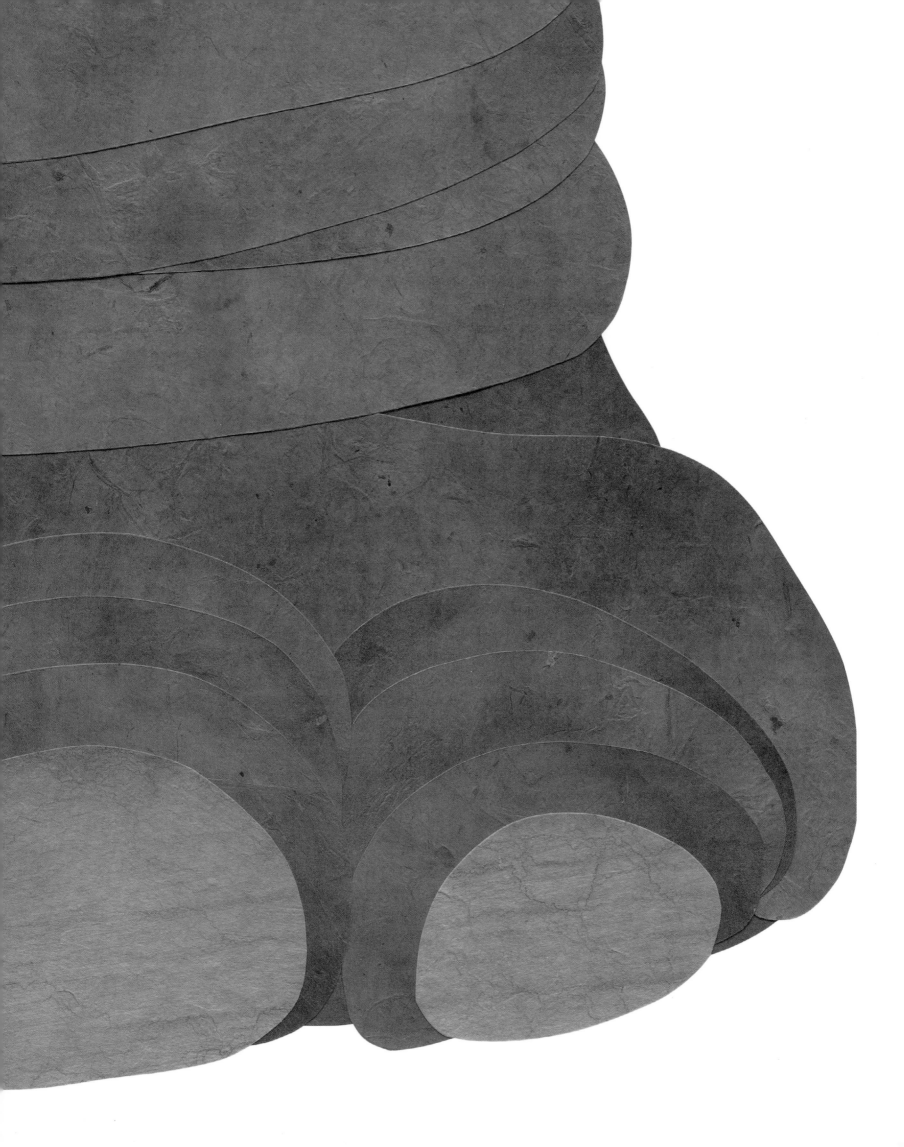

The **pygmy shrew** has a body just 5 centimetres long and weighs less than a 10 pence piece. This tiny rodent lives in the mountains and forests of North America. The pygmy shrew consumes twice its own weight in food each day and is a fierce predator. It will eat almost anything it can catch and kill, including earthworms, insects, spiders and small frogs.

The **giant squid** is a mysterious creature that has never been seen alive. The largest giant squid ever recorded was found dead in the waters off New Zealand. With its tentacles, it measured over 18 metres in length and weighed more than 900 kilograms. These animals are relatives of the octopus and live in water 200 to 900 metres deep, where they probably eat fish, shrimp and other squid, which they capture with their two long feeder tentacles. They bite their prey into small pieces with a large, parrot-like beak. Giant squid have eyes the size of basketballs, the largest of any animal. Giant squid are a favourite food of sperm whales. The whales and squid must have terrific battles deep in the ocean – sperm whales are often found with huge round scars caused by the suckers on the squid's tentacles.

The **atlas moth** got its name because the patterns on its wings reminded people of maps. It is the largest moth, with wings up to 30 centimetres across. The atlas moth lives in Southeast Asia, where its large cocoons are sometimes made into purses by the local people. The black spots on the tips of the atlas moth's wings are called eye spots. They make the wing tips look like snake heads, which may scare away predators. These moths feed on nectar from flowers in the rainforests where they live.

Growing to about 9 millimetres in length, the **dwarf goby**, the world's smallest fish, lives in the coral reefs of the western Pacific Ocean. It would take 250 dwarf gobies to weigh one gram. Female gobies attach their eggs to coral or rocks, where the males guard them until they hatch.

The largest meat-eating animal that lives on land is the **Alaskan brown bear**. When it stands on its hind legs, it can be more than 4 metres tall, and it weighs as much as 770 kilograms. Despite its size, this bear can run at 55 kilometres per hour for short distances – faster than a horse. It makes its home in the arctic regions of the world and eats seeds, berries, insects and small mammals. Sometimes brown bears eat larger animals, such as elk or moose. The Alaskan brown bear's favourite food is salmon, which it catches by standing in fast-moving rivers and grabbing the fish in its jaws or swatting them up on to the bank with its huge paws.

The **ostrich** can't fly, but it can run at speeds of around 65 kilometres per hour. Standing up to 2·75 metres tall and weighing 155 kilograms, it is the largest living bird. Ostriches live in groups, or flocks, which often mingle with herds of zebras and other grazing animals in Africa. The herds stir up the insects and small mammals that the ostriches eat, and the ostriches warn of approaching lions or hyenas. If necessary, the ostrich can defend itself against predators with powerful kicks of its legs. The ostrich egg, which weighs almost 1·5 kilograms, is the largest egg of any animal.

The **giant anteater** has no teeth in its long, narrow mouth. It uses its sticky 60-centimetre-long tongue to eat up to 30 000 ants or termites a day, crushing them against the roof of its mouth. This anteater has long, curved claws on its front feet which it uses to tear open insect nests. It doesn't completely destroy the colonies of the insects it attacks, though. It leaves enough ants or termites behind to rebuild their nests. Including its bushy tail, the giant anteater can be up to 2·5 metres in length and weigh up to 40 kilograms. Giant anteaters make their home in the forests and grasslands of Central and South America. They are a favourite food of jaguars, but can defend themselves by standing up on their back legs and striking out with their claws. Anteaters have poor vision but a very good sense of smell.

The **Goliath birdeater tarantula**, with legs that can span 30 centimetres, is the largest spider in the world. It lives in burrows in the soft floor of South American forests, leaping out to grab insects, frogs, lizards, birds and small mammals. Like most spiders, it kills or paralyses its prey by injecting venom with its fangs. Birdeaters sometimes bite people, but luckily for us their bite isn't serious – it causes only mild pain, like a bee sting. Spiders don't have teeth to tear up their prey. Instead, they dribble digestive juices on to their victims, then suck up their meal. Birdeaters also have the ability, unusual among spiders, to make sound. They create a soft hissing noise by rubbing the hairs on their legs together. They can also defend themselves by releasing hairs from their body. These tiny hairs are very irritating to the skin, eyes and mouths of other animals.

The **saltwater crocodile** is the world's largest reptile. It grows up to 7 metres long and weighs as much as 900 kilograms. Saltwater crocodiles, which can live in both fresh and salt water, are found in the rivers and coastal areas of Australia and Southeast Asia, where they eat fish, birds, monkeys, buffalo and livestock. This crocodile will float motionless for hours, waiting for an animal to come to the water's edge. It then slips under the water and quietly swims toward its intended victim. When it is close enough, strokes of its powerful tail launch it from the water. The crocodile grabs its prey in its 60-centimetre-long jaws and drags it back into the water, where the animal is held under until it drowns. Saltwater crocodiles can stay under water for more than an hour and have been seen swimming in the ocean as far as 950 kilometres from land. Along with their relatives the alligators, crocodiles kill more people around the world than any other animal.

The world's largest frog is the **Goliath frog** of western Africa. From nose to toes, this frog is almost 90 centimetres long. It weighs as much as 3 kilograms, about the same as a domestic cat. Goliath frogs eat insects, other frogs and amphibians, and sometimes small mammals. Like all frogs, they don't drink water – they absorb it through their skin. These frogs are silent. They have no vocal sac, so they can't croak.

Many people think the **great white shark** is the scariest animal on earth. This fierce predator can be more than 6·5 metres long and weigh 2700 kilograms. Though it has been known to attack and kill humans, it prefers to eat seals, sea lions and fish. In fact, great whites that attack people often spit them out after taking a bite. They have as many as 3000 teeth, which are arranged in several rows. When a tooth breaks or falls out, one from the next row moves up to take its place. The shark is an ancient animal – it has looked much the same for more than 400 million years. These efficient hunters have a very good sense of smell and use special organs to detect the electrical fields of fish and other animals.

The smallest primate (and one of the smallest mammals) is the **pygmy mouse lemur**. This rare tree-dwelling creature has a body which is only about 6 centimetres long and weighs less than 30 grams. It lives in the forests of Madagascar, an island off the eastern coast of Africa. Lemurs eat fruit, flowers and nectar. They sleep during the day and are active at night, using their large eyes to help them feed and move about.

The **gorilla**, found in the forests of central Africa, is an endangered animal. People have shot and captured so many gorillas that they are in danger of becoming extinct in the wild. These gentle but powerful animals are the largest primates, a group that includes the lemurs, monkeys and great apes. The males stand 1·65 to 1·8 metres tall and can weigh as much as 270 kilograms. Gorillas are very intelligent animals that live in tight-knit social groups. They are attentive parents, playing with their babies and teaching them how to find food and get along with others in their group. Gorillas are vegetarians, eating leaves, fruit, nuts and roots.

**Siberian tigers**, the largest of all cats, are found in the forests of one small part of Russia. These tigers are in great danger of becoming extinct – there are only a few hundred left in the wild. Siberian tigers can be up to 4·25 metres long (including their tail) and weigh more than 320 kilograms. They are stealthy and powerful predators, able to leap 9 metres in a single bound. These tigers hunt wild pigs, deer and elk, though they will eat frogs, snakes and small mammals – even porcupines – if larger prey can't be found.

The **Goliath beetle** is the world's heaviest insect. Found in the rainforests of central Africa, it is up to 15 centimetres long and can weigh over 100 grams. This beetle is harmless to humans and is often kept as a pet in Japan and other countries. It feeds on dead plant material and dung.

The largest animal living on land is the **African elephant**. Elephants are endangered – they have long been hunted for their ivory tusks, and much of the African forest and grassland where they live has been turned into farmland. A male African elephant can stand 4 metres tall at the shoulder and weigh as much as 6350 kilograms. These sensitive and intelligent animals live in groups and feed on grass, shrubs and trees. An elephant eats several hundred kilograms of vegetation a day and feeds almost constantly when not sleeping. One of the elephant's most unusual features is its long, sensitive trunk, which it uses to eat, drink, defend itself and care for its young. With its trunk, an elephant can tear down a tree or pick up an egg without breaking it.

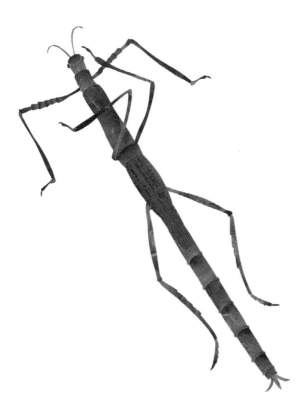

**Giant walking stick** insects are found in many parts of the world. The largest kind of giant walking stick is found in Indonesia, a group of islands in the western Pacific Ocean. One of these measured 56 centimetres long, easily making it the longest insect in the world. Walking sticks are gentle, slow-moving insects that feed on plants. When motionless, they look almost exactly like a twig or branch. This camouflage helps protect them from birds and other predators.

The world's largest earthworm can be found in one small part of Australia. The **giant Gippsland earthworm** grows to more than 90 centimetres in length and 25 millimetres in diameter. It lives in a complex system of burrows, where it eats roots and plant material in the soil. Earthworms move by stretching out the front of their body, then pulling up the back part. This motion creates a sucking noise that can be heard above the ground as the giant earthworm crawls through its underground tunnels.

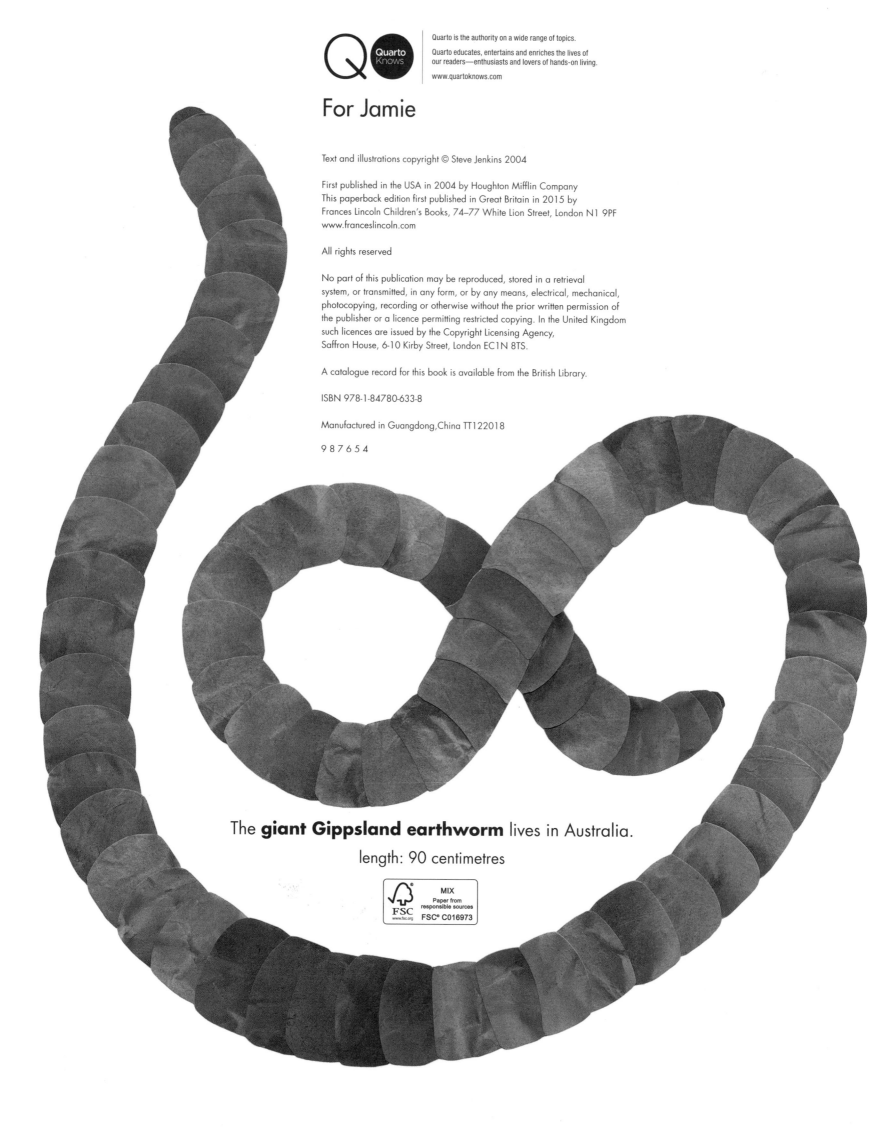

Quarto is the authority on a wide range of topics.
Quarto educates, entertains and enriches the lives of
our readers—enthusiasts and lovers of hands-on living.
www.quartoknows.com

For Jamie

Text and illustrations copyright © Steve Jenkins 2004

First published in the USA in 2004 by Houghton Mifflin Company
This paperback edition first published in Great Britain in 2015 by
Frances Lincoln Children's Books, 74–77 White Lion Street, London N1 9PF
www.franceslincoln.com

A catalogue record for this book is available from the British Library.

ISBN 978-1-84780-633-8

Manufactured in Guangdong,China TT122018

9 8 7 6 5 4

The **giant Gippsland earthworm** lives in Australia.

length: 90 centimetres